TRYTHIS!
Baking

Stephanie Turnbull

A+
Smart Apple Media

Published by Smart Apple Media, an imprint of Black Rabbit Books
P.O. Box 3263, Mankato, Minnesota, 56002
www.blackrabbitbooks.com

Printed in the United States of America, at Corporate Graphics
in North Mankato, Minnesota.

Designed and illustrated by Guy Callaby
Edited by Mary-Jane Wilkins

Cataloging-in-Publication Data is available from the Library of Congress

ISBN 978-1-62588-370-4

Photo acknowledgements
t = top, b = bottom, l = left, r = right, c = center
page 1 vetasster; 3 Shebeko; 4 Simone van den Berg; 5t antpkr,
l Africa Studio, r Roxana Bashyrova, b Andrea Skjold/all Shutterstock;
7, 9 Mim Waller; 11 Olga Nayashkova/Shutterstock; 13, 15, 17, 19,
21 Mim Waller; 22 Andrey Starostin; 23 Madlen/both Shutterstock
Cover top right Timmary/Shutterstock, main image Fuse/Thinkstock

DAD0062
022015
9 8 7 6 5 4 3 2 1

Contents

Why try baking?

Baking is a fantastic hobby. Here are a few reasons to try it!

It's fun to try out recipes and experiment with different ingredients.

1 It's easy to do.
Anyone can bake—the secret is to stick to simple recipes, measure ingredients exactly, and don't let things overcook! Ask an adult to help with hot stoves and ovens.

2 There's so much to try.
How about baking a pasta meal, making your own bread and pizza, or trying out delicious muffins, cakes, and cookies?

3 Home baking is good for you.
Home-made food is far fresher than shop-bought stuff, and you can fill it with plenty of healthy extras such as fruit and nuts.

4 The food tastes amazing!
Testing out your baking is fun—why not invite your friends over and have a food-tasting party? Make your favorite things, or invent your own recipes.

Now test out the brilliant projects in this book and see for yourself how much fun baking can be.
Look for the helpful tips and extra ideas.

Macaroni bake

A pasta bake makes a perfect hot, filling dinner. If you make too much, put the rest in the freezer.

You will need:
1 butternut squash
1 tbsp olive oil
salt and pepper
10 oz (300g) macaroni
2 oz (50g) butter
2 oz (50g) plain flour
1 tsp Chinese or Dijon mustard
17 fluid oz (500 ml) milk
7 oz (200g) cheddar cheese, grated
2 oz (50g) grated **Parmesan** cheese

Serves 4

Have all your ingredients ready before making the sauce. It will go lumpy if you don't keep stirring.

1 *Heat the oven to 400°F (200°C). Deseed, slice, peel, and chop the squash. Lay the chunks on a baking tray and coat them with the oil.* **Season**, *then bake for 20-25 minutes until soft.*

2 *Cook the* **macaroni** *in a big pan of boiling, salted water.*

3 *Melt the butter in a pan,* **sift** *in the flour, add the mustard, and stir to a smooth paste. Take it off the heat.*

4 *Slowly mix in the milk, whisking if there are lumps. Put it back on the heat and bring to a boil, stirring.*

5 *Take off the heat and mash in a third of the squash. Stir in the cheddar and half the Parmesan. Season, then stir in the macaroni and the rest of the squash.*

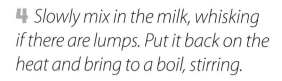

6 *Spread into a large ovenproof dish and sprinkle the rest of the Parmesan on top. Bake for 15 minutes or until golden and bubbling on top.*

Now try this
Try adding sliced sausage or chicken to your bake, or use different pasta.

Bread rolls

Warm, freshly baked bread tastes great, and it isn't hard to make.

You will need:

1lb 2 oz (500g) bread flour (white or whole wheat)

¼ oz (7g) package fast-action **yeast**

1½ tsp sugar

2 tsp salt

½ pint (300 ml) warm water

3 tbsp olive oil

Makes 8 rolls

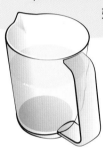

1 Sift the flour into a big bowl. Stir in the yeast, sugar, and salt. Make a hollow in the middle.

2 Pour the warm water and oil into the hollow. Gradually stir in the flour with a wooden spoon.

3 When the mixture turns into a sticky dough, mold it into a ball with your hands.

4 **Knead** the bread for 10 minutes on a floury surface, pushing it down and folding it over until it's soft and stretchy.

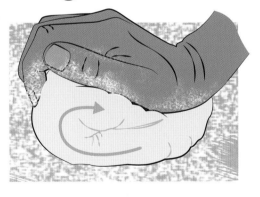

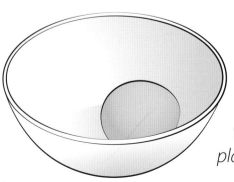

5 Put the dough in the bowl, cover with a dish towel and stand in a warm place for an hour. It will double in size!

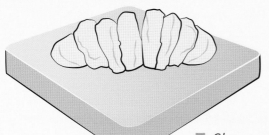

6 *Knead the dough for a few minutes, roll it into a sausage and cut into 8 pieces.*

7 *Shape each piece into a ball and place on a **greased** baking tray. Cover and leave for another hour, then bake in an oven heated to 400°F (200°C).*

Allow time for the dough to rise twice.

8 *Bake for 12-15 minutes, until pale brown. If the rolls sound hollow when you tap the base, they're ready.*

Take the rolls out of the oven when they're still pale, otherwise they'll overcook.

Now try this

Make special rolls by adding a sprinkle of dried herbs, chopped sun-dried tomatoes, or seeds to the dough.

Pizza

Make a base from bread dough then add sauce, cheese, and toppings to create your own pizza!

You will need:
bread dough ingredients (see page 8)
1 onion
3 cloves garlic
2 tbsp olive oil
14 oz (400g) can chopped tomatoes
1 tbsp tomato paste
1 tsp dried oregano
salt and pepper
mozzarella cheese and toppings

Serves 4

1 *Follow steps 1-5 on page 8 to make dough, divide into four, and roll out into circles on a floury surface. Lay the pieces on greased baking trays.*

Make them about ½ inch (1½ cm) thick.

2 *Peel and chop the onion and garlic, then fry in the oil for five minutes, stirring.*

3 Add the tomatoes, tomato paste, and oregano. Season, mix, and **simmer**, covered, for half an hour.

4 Let the sauce cool, then smooth a couple of tablespoons over each base.

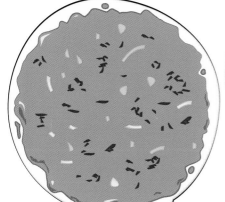

Keep sauce away from the edges, or it may burn.

5 Cover with a layer of sliced mozzarella cheese then add a few toppings, such as olives, ham, pepperoni, mushrooms, cherry tomatoes, tuna, or peppers.

6 Bake in an oven heated to 400°F (200°C) for about 12 minutes.

Now try this

Try more unusual toppings: how about figs and blue cheese, avocado and prawns, or pears and walnuts?

Yogurt muffins

These easy muffins make great snacks —they're full of fruit and not too sweet.

You will need:
5 oz (150g) container flavored yogurt
¾ container sunflower oil
1 container caster sugar
3 container self-raising flour
1 container chopped, dried fruit
1 egg
½ container milk

Makes 12 muffins

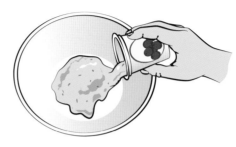

1 Empty the yogurt into a mixing bowl. Rinse out the container.

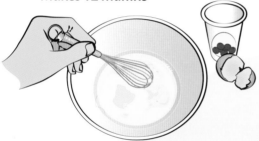

2 Measure the oil in the container and add it to the bowl. Break in an egg, add the milk, then whisk well.

3 Mix in the sugar with a wooden spoon.

4 Sift in the flour, then mix.

5 Stir in the dried fruit. Cranberries, apricots, and raisins work well.

6 Grease a muffin pan and spoon the mixture into each cup.

 Put the same amount of mixture in each muffin cup.

Now try this

In a pan, gently heat 2 oz (55g) butter, 3½ oz (100g) powdered sugar, the juice of a lemon and 2 tablespoons hot water. Whisk the mixture, then dip in your muffins to coat them with a tasty lemon **glaze**.

7 Bake for 15 minutes at 350ºF (180ºC), or until pale brown and springy. Leave for a few minutes, then remove with a spatula and cool on a wire rack.

Choc chip cookies

These soft, chewy cookies taste great served warm with a glass of cold milk.

You will need:
4 oz (115g) butter
5½ oz (155g) light brown sugar
½ tsp vanilla extract
1 large egg
8 oz (225g) white flour
3½ oz (100g) dark chocolate

Makes about 14 cookies

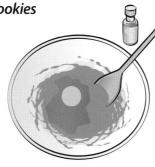
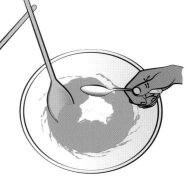

1 *Chop the butter in a bowl, add the sugar, and mix with a wooden spoon until creamy.*

2 *Add the vanilla, break in the egg, and **beat** until light and fluffy.*

3 *Sift the flour into another bowl and add it gradually to the mixture, stirring it in gently.*

4 *Chop or break the chocolate into chunks, then mix in.*

5 Use your hands to make golf ball-sized lumps of dough, then flatten them. Place them on a baking tray lined with parchment paper.

Cookies spread as they bake, so don't put them too close together.

6 Bake for 12-15 minutes at 350ºF (180ºC), until the cookies are pale golden brown. Move to a wire rack to cool.

Now try this
Try using white chocolate or nuts, or use white sugar and plain flour for crispier, crunchier cookies.

Banana bars

Bought cereal bars are often full of sugar, so it's more healthy— and fun—to make your own.

You will need:
3 large, ripe bananas
9 oz (250g) rolled oats
1 tsp cinnamon
2 oz (50g) butter
3 tbsp dark corn syrup

Makes 12 bars

1 *Melt the butter in a small pan.*

2 *Put the oats, cinnamon, corn syrup, and melted butter in a large mixing bowl. Stir well.*

3 *Mash the bananas in another bowl, then add to the oat mixture. Stir with a metal spoon.*

Dark corn syrup helps the mixture stick together, so add more if your mixture seems dry.

4 Line a small, rectangular baking tray with parchment paper. Pour in the mixture and press it down evenly with the back of a wet spoon.

5 Bake for 20-25 minutes at 400°F (200°C), until the top is golden. Leave to cool in the tray, then cut into 12 rectangles.

Oat bars are great lunchbox treats and after-school snacks, or try them with yogurt for breakfast.

Now try this

Invent your own bars! Use one banana and 7 oz (200g) oats, then add handfuls of dried fruit, seeds, chopped nuts, grated apple, or puffed rice cereal.

Carrot cake

Carrots contain natural sugar and taste sweet but not *too* sweet.

You will need:
4 oz (125g) self-rising flour
pinch salt
1 tsp cinnamon
4 oz (125g) soft brown sugar
2 large eggs
3 fl oz (100ml) sunflower oil
1 large carrot
1 oz (25g) shredded coconut
1 oz (25g) chopped walnuts

For the icing:
1 oz (25g) butter
7 oz (200g) powdered sugar
3½ oz (100g) cream cheese
½ tsp vanilla extract

1 Sift the flour into a large mixing bowl. Add the salt, cinnamon, and sugar. Stir to mix.

2 Measure the oil in a large mixing cup, then break in the eggs. Beat, then pour into the bowl and mix.

3 Peel and grate the carrot into a bowl, then add to the mixture with the coconut and walnuts. Stir.

Graters are sharp–don't grate your fingers!

**4** *Line a large rectangular cake pan with parchment paper. Pour in the mixture so it fills the pan evenly. Bake at 350°F (180°C) for about 20 minutes.*

5 *Leave to cool in the pan, then move to a wire rack. Make the icing: beat the butter until smooth, sift in the icing sugar, and stir in the cream cheese and vanilla.*

6 *Spread the icing over the cake with the back of a spoon. Cut into slices and decorate each with a piece of walnut.*

Now try this
Flavor the icing with maple syrup or lemon juice instead of vanilla.

Chocolate pudding

This delicious dessert magically separates into soft sponge cake and thick rich sauce as it bakes.

You will need:
2 oz (50g) butter
3 oz (75g) sugar
2 large eggs
1½ oz (40g) self-rising flour
5 tsp cocoa powder
1½ cups (350 ml) milk

1 *Chop the butter into a mixing bowl. Add the sugar and beat with a wooden spoon until fluffy.*

2 *Crack an egg over a bowl, catching the yolk in half the shell while the white runs into the bowl. Move the yolk from one half of the shell to the other to drain off the white, then add the yolk to the butter and sugar. Do the same with the other egg.*

Be careful not to drop the egg yolks or let them break.

3 *Beat in the yolks with the wooden spoon.*

4 *Sift in the flour and cocoa powder and beat until well mixed.*

5 Gradually add the milk, whisking gently to prevent lumps.

6 Use an electric beater to beat the egg whites into a thick white foam.

7 **Fold** the whites gently into the mixture, keeping it as airy and fluffy as possible.

8 Pour into a greased ovenproof bowl. Bake for 35-40 minutes at 350°F (180°C), until the top is set and spongy.

Now try this

Try making individual chocolate puddings in small, ovenproof bowls. Serve to your friends!

Glossary

beat
To stir or whip up ingredients quickly, adding air to make them light and fluffy.

fold
To mix gently, lifting the mixture carefully with a spoon so it stays light and airy.

glaze
A glossy, usually sweet coating for baked foods. Glazes are often made from powdered sugar, eggs, or milk.

greased
Smeared with a thin layer of butter or cooking margarine. Greasing a tray stops food from sticking to it in the oven.

knead
To press and mold a mixture with your hands to work it into a smooth dough.

macaroni
Pasta shaped into short tubes, which can be straight or curved.

mozzarella
A rubbery, white Italian cheese. It's great for pizzas because it becomes soft and gooey when melted.

Parmesan
A hard, dry Italian cheese, usually served grated over food.

season
To add salt and pepper to food to improve the taste. Sprinkle in a little of each, then taste the food to see if it needs more.

macaroni

sift

To put flour or other dry ingredients through fine mesh to get rid of any lumps.

simmer

To keep a liquid cooking gently. Let it boil first, then turn down the heat until there are hardly any bubbles.

yeast

A fungus that turns the sugar in a dough mixture into gas, making air bubbles. Without yeast, bread is flat and hard. It's usually sold as granules in packs and starts to work when warmed, so always make sure your water isn't cold—but not boiling hot, either.

Web sites

www.cookinglight.com/food/basic-baking-skills
Learn useful baking skills and find out more about basic ingredients.

www.allrecipes.co.uk/recipes/tag-5485/muffins-for-kids-recipes.aspx
Discover how to make any type of muffin you can imagine!

www.kidshealth.org/kid/recipes
Find fun, healthy recipes for people who can't eat certain foods.

Index